www.finishinglinepress.com

BORDER SONGS:
A Conversation in Poems

poems by

Ona Gritz and Daniel Simpson

Finishing Line Press
Georgetown, Kentucky

BORDER SONGS:
A Conversation in Poems

ACKNOWLEDGMENTS

We would like to thank the editors of the following publications in which some
of these poems have appeared:

The American Voice: "In Rockaway"
Atlanta Review: "Acts of Faith"
Bellevue Literary Review: "Hemiplegia II" as "Hemiplegia"
Disability Studies Quarterly: "Vigilance and Dissembling"
Lilith: "Exodus"
Lily: "Ignoring the Apples"
The Pedestal Magazine: "Abraham's Hand"
Ploughshares: "Retelling"
Tiferet: "When the Man You Love Is a Blind Man"
Wordgathering: "A Blind Boy's First Glimpse of Heaven," "My Excuse," "When We
Were Four," "There among the Haves," and "First Anniversary"

Publisher: Leah Maines

Editor: Christen Kincaid

Cover Art: Juan Alberto Pérez

Author Photo: Naomi Ages

Cover Design: Elizabeth Maines McCleavy

Printed in the USA on acid-free paper.
Order online: www.finishinglinepress.com
        also available on amazon.com

Author inquiries and mail orders:
Finishing Line Press
P. O. Box 1626
Georgetown, Kentucky 40324
U. S. A.

Table of Contents

To Stephen Dunn and Peter Murphy who, just by carrying out their commitment to poetry, unwittingly brought us together.

When We Were Four

and my twin brother and I got to jumping
on our twin mattresses,
which had lain in boredom on their wooden frames,
we put our agitators in overdrive,
turned our beds into washing machines.
Steam climbed up the wall behind our headboards.
It's hard work shaking the footboard
fast enough to spin-dry a full load.
We seem to have been the first in Berwyn, Pennsylvania
to discover you could do this.
Grampappy Armstrong just clicked his tongue.
Were we the work of the devil?
I told myself I was not afraid of the devil,
but my fear of the devil tasted like horseradish,
and my shame like the smell of sour milk.
Down the street lived a dog named Satan,
who used to shit in our front yard,
and every time my Welsh grandmother said *iechyd da*
right after the grace, it would make me laugh.
Danny Boy could laugh at anything.
We were as quiet as squirrels.
We couldn't sit still at the table
because we had plastic plates and cups
and our chairs had their backs to the wall.
"Father had the shipfitter blues," we bellowed
as the sharp needle of innocence
played through the old 78 of evening
and we trampolined into the limbs of old oaks,
bouncing harder and higher each time,
hoping to stave off night and the ghost of the puppy
who had once fallen through our wild arms.
Venez, vivez avec nous, said the leaves,
promising that stars would bathe us and the sun would dress us.
Gutten nacht, said shirts from a laundry basket,
and the bed slept, holding hands with the water pipes.

Retelling

The sun was nothing more than an orange
the day Lisa ran for the ice cream truck.
It was small and even if it held sweetness,
even if it seeped Vitamin C, it couldn't stop
the car from barreling down Mott Avenue,
couldn't shine enough to show the driver
the seven year old girl dashing in front of his
Pontiac so that his foot would choose the brake.
The trees that saw it happen were no more
than rakes upended. They had no leaves
to form shadows. They had no song.
For a long moment, doorknobs
were merely ornamental. Those of us still
in our houses stayed in our houses.
I, five at the time, kept watching cartoons
while the sun watched over us and the trees
turned into notebooks so the story could change.

Visitations of Abandonment

It came again, that same dream
trip down 95 to Florida,
all the motels full so far,
my mother asleep in the passenger seat,
my father still driving since five this morning,
me making him talk every minute or two
("How's the traffic? ... Any motels lately?"),
until some question goes unanswered
(was it "Where are we now?"),
and I say, "Dad ... Dad? ..."

(just tires humming, that's all—
not even the radio crackling
over a fading station).
I reach up, touch
the empty seat, the orphaned steering wheel,
and though I am blind and only eight
and know nothing of driving or physics,
my bowels can calculate
mass times rate of speed.
I have never felt a road so smooth.

Hemiplegia I

I was maybe five when I first tried
to make sense of it, my split self,
the side that recognizes everything it touches,
the side that feels muted, slept on.
Why do I feel less on the right?
I wondered aloud and with the swiftness
of someone who's been waiting to be asked,
my mom said, *Your heart's on the left.*
Like everyone's. We were headed somewhere
in our blue Barracuda, my father focused
on the road, my mother gazing out
the passenger window as she defined the world.
I sat in back, the middle spot, feet on the hump,
left hand feeling for the ordinary drumbeat
I shared with every other living soul,
right not feeling much of anything at all.

A Blind Boy's First Glimpse of Heaven

I climbed the stepladder to Heaven when I was eight,
my father spotting me from behind.
I liked that he stayed below.
How else could I hear where the world was?

"You can move around, Son, but shuffle your feet,
in case there's a stray bale of hay to trip over,
and you don't want to walk off the edge."

God was in a meeting, I guess.
Anyway, I never saw Him.
What had He done to Lucifer?
And what did the Bible mean by "cast him out?"

Did God have a squad of angel goons up there
to blindside him from the back and shove him off?
I wanted to jump, to see if I'd survive.

Fifty years later, Aunt Polly said,
"You better get ready, Dan, if you want God
to take you up to be with your dad again,
and won't it be great to finally see his face?"

I don't know. I'm just getting to love
this world for what it is, a flawed place
with its subway platforms overlooking the third rail,
its hay lofts, open sewers and loading docks,
and all the strangers who've looked out for me,
letting me take their arms to walk with them.

I'm thinking, the next time I see Aunt Polly,
I'm going to tell her about my new vision:
"It's really going to be something," I'll say.
"In Heaven, you'll finally get to be blind."

In Rockaway

I have been out of the water
three years, breathing air.
They have placed me waist deep,
my bottom hanging in the familiar wet
like a conch shell.
Beside me, standing rooted and tall,
father, uncle.
I do not yet know they are brothers.
I do not yet know I am here
because one of them entered water,
pulled me out.
In front of us water lifts
like a greedy tongue that could take me back.
I yell, "Over my head, it's over my head"
and the men laugh,
raise me by the arms
into the air between them.
I think it's magic to be lifted whole-bodied,
magic that they do it each time, saving my life.
I do not yet know this is my element,
run, like I am, by the moon.
I do not yet know I will come here,
sucking the salt from my hair,
loving the slap of waves on my bones,
letting it drip with a tap down my back.
I do not yet know I will come here
in dark hours with other men,
finding the water
I began collecting inside me on this day,
making it rise, dance, begin to seep.

Ocean Romance

Until today it seemed
only others connected like this
at fast-food stands in train stations
or outside juice bars on the boardwalk
and felt summer open into another country.

But now it is we who are walking in together, hand in hand,
reporting by shrieks the moment of shock
when the water freezes our genitals.

The undertow is strong this cloudless night.
There are no lifeguards here—no one else
except two far-off surfers trying to catch
the edge of an augured hurricane,
which seems as unreal to me
as the Messiah in Sunday school.

"Never fuck with Mother Nature," you laugh
when I begin taunting the ocean.
And then you out-shout me:
"Is that all you have? That's the best you can do?"
How can, so soon, I be carrying you,
your bare back and legs like liquid
all over my arms and chest?

You have your eyes on the moon. Even now,
it is calling you through cycles
in ways it can't call me.
Whose babies will come out of you like stars,
if not mine?

If I hold to you this way,
will I feel the tide?
"Dish out everything," I'm thinking,
"everything you've got."

Someday, maybe, even on dry land
we will splash each other's shoulders
with our own salt water,
our eyes cleansed and clear.
People have died in here
hoping for a lot less.

Border Song

Yaj cured me of my taste
for bad boys when we kissed
at our tenth grade beach party,
someone's staticy transistor
ruining an Elton John song,
the crackling bonfire
giving our clothes and hair
a sweet burnt smell.
Later, he bragged to his friends
that my nipples grew hard
when he grazed them
like it was his sloppy tongue
and not the ocean chill
that made them into little beads.
I wrote his real name, *Jay*,
in the sand with a stick
and erased it, then wandered
to the water's lacy edge.
Away from the others,
I wondered how it felt to kiss
a boy and *feel* something, how
it felt to kiss a boy who mattered.
High school's half over!
kids shouted, dancing
in the orange light of the fire.
I half wanted to go back
to that first untouched September.
I half wanted all of this
to hurry up and end.

All Day, New Friends

Massachusetts Youth Hostel, Summer of '99

We three rode in the back seat
of Larry's '88 Impala,
you on my left, Karen on my right, naked
except for our bathing suits and sandals,
Larry driving (it being his car) and singing
with Paul to an REM tape on tiny speakers
while we three talked about who smoked
grass, and when, and what it was like, and Marijuana brownies,
and the difference between them and smoking,
our warm knees and thighs, hips and arms
rearranging themselves against one another,
as we jangled over ruts and potholes,
jangling memories and wishes loose,
so that I, knowing we were one day old together
and tomorrow this would end, said,
my breathing feeling thick, "Where were you all,
you and Karen and Paul and Larry, when
I was in high school, the first blind kid
trying to hear a few friends in the Pep Club's
Thanksgiving Eve bonfire crowd,
trying to find his way to a party
of the coolest classmates, where were you?"
which prompted Karen to say, "Yeah,
it would have been great," and you, you on my left,
to say, "Hey, what about playing basketball,
can we do that? I mean there must be a way
we can figure that out."

Eighteen

We never spoke of what my body
couldn't do, so when Jen and Kay
left to pick apricots from the spindly tree
behind the library, I hesitated.
But Rich would be there.
I showed up in a wraparound skirt,
my excuse to stand at the base,
pluck from the bottom branch.
The fruit was concentrated at the top.
While the others climbed, of course
it was Rich I watched, squinting
up at him as I had all summer.
The night before, he'd finally
kissed me, his tongue tentatively
grazing my own. Catch, he called
now and I lifted my skirt to form
a net, no thought to palsy, to exposing
my uneven legs. When the first
tangy oval dropped into the voile
I had already begun to taste it,
how it felt to be chosen. And whole.

My Excuse

I lit the candles, poured the wine.
You were hungry, too,
in that college room,
but for something more permanent than I.

I was still too much the young boy,
made to sleep in an open dorm,
desire and curiosity stoked
by years of being forced to play
on a cold, northern playground,
separate from the girls.

You had dreams that expanded into deep time.
All I wanted was a generous friend
in a narrow bed in a closet of a room.

Love, or so I called you then,
can you give me a free pass?
I say I only wanted
something safe and narrow,
and yet, on some blind level,
I saw the rightness of the wide and deep you hoped for –

what I hoped for,
when I sweet-talked the housemother
as I snuck a radio into the dorm.

I thought I might get lucky
and catch a wave of love song
from some station in the sun-soaked South,
a wave that would sweep me across the playground
and over its high brick wall.

Hemiplegia II

Left, my bright half, gets all of it...
soft sharp prickly wet lined.
But press your head against my right shoulder,
I sense weight but no warmth. Your cheek,
to my right touch, stubble free,
whether or not you shave.
Under my right fingers your silver hair
holds no silk, nor can I feel it part
into single strands. I'll tell you
how I know you in the dark.
Left whispers the details.
Right listens and believes.

Vigilance and Dissembling

Since I don't see, and have no visual cues,
I'm fascinated by how sighted people dissemble.
I bet they keep their faces unflustered,
while behind their stationary eyes
another set of eyes checks you out.

I say this because, in conversation,
I try to act undivided
while, in fact, I'm on alert
for any glitch in composure,
any revelation of an actor playing a part.

It's often a matter of tone of voice.
Most people don't realize it goes even further—
that I'm listening to them breathe,
that I hear body language.
Someone talking with her right hand,
while I hold her left,
doesn't know how much I know
from the way her body moves,
as if she never touched a tie-line to a dock
and guessed the boat was bobbing up and down.

When the Man You Love Is a Blind Man

You can stop shaving your legs
when the temperature drops
and he'll say he likes a change
in texture with the seasons. You can
leave that bit of silver in your bangs.
Your fashion advice will be gospel.
When he tells you you're beautiful,
you'll know he's talking about
something in you that's timeless,
something about you that's true.
If, teasing, he says that smearing color
on your face is what a clown does,
explain how a touch of blush
can change the feel of entering a room
and he'll listen. He'll always listen
like the wide world is a raft with only
two people on it and he finds you
the more interesting of the two.
Imagine going with him to the Rockies.
He hears you sigh and asks
what the mountains look like. All you have
are words. *Awesome. Grandeur.*
But when you describe that feeling
of seeing your one life for the flicker it is,
he knows. *Oh*, he says. *Oh.*
It's like hearing music in a cathedral.

Listening to New York Radio in the Middle of the Night

There, in insomniac City
where the dial can easily hold
five languages beyond English
and stations bleed into each other,
Emily Dickinson—satisfied
she could no longer see to see—
spoke through a piano
while a Spanish man, half-crying,
half singing, declared he too
would die if the one he most
desired did not give him
her undying love.
Between Emily and the Spanish man,
a sitar spoke harmoniously
about rock-steady faith,
while picking its way along
a path of dissonant doubt.
Commercial life finally
put to bed, Lennon
woke up from a good dream,
his imagination intact.
He sang with the sitar, calling
the chutney and raita left over
from last night's dinner to put on
spiritual livery.
They in turn inspired
the beans in my cabinet
to take on a holy presence,
and the cabinets themselves,
dazed at first, recalled
the distant spirits of trees.
And when the whole house became
tuned like this to the radio,

my father kindly caught
a coach from that other kingdom
to sit in my living room,
if only for a moment,
and casually talk with me
of ordinary life.

Donner Lake

I chose the still mirror of this lake.
Clean sky preening above it,
redwoods doubling green.

The hungry name, ancient history
and sudden winter. This was August.
From the radio, John Lennon

asked us, imagine no heaven.
We let your heavy ashes go.
First smoke, then silt.

If you had some other place
in mind, you never said.
Or, I wasn't listening just then.

My Pants Are Drenched with Rain

My pants are drenched with rain,
which came sideways and up my legs
as I walked home from the bus.

Once, Jenny filled my hand with hers
as we walked in the drizzle.
Her hands were wide and quiet—
hands that could listen,
quiet like a priest at confession.

My father's hands were busy,
not soft and uncaloused like mine.
I touched all the caskets before I chose
a pine box that was smooth and lean—
no nicks or splinters like the rocking boat
he hammered together for me in the cellar.
I picked a pine box and the sun poured down.

But now, my pants are drenched with rain.
May there be no time this weekend—
no time and not too much sun.
May there be no more train whistles
saying you must go somewhere,
and none of the usual loneliness.

I have other pants, dry pants,
that would match the red shirt with the swan,
the one I have on.

I am rich; my ears are full of talk.
Once, my arms were full of someone half my age.
Her shirt was filling up with water
and yet she breathed air in and out.
She did this repeatedly and without effort.
Everything she did amazed me.

Pretty soon, I will be dry.
Will the memory of my father fade
the way rain evaporates?

My mind is full of words.
I have not run out of things to say.
I make emphatic statements about the future and the present:
"Jesus shall reign" and "the rain it raineth every day."

How many years of rain
make dust of a wooden coffin?

One week after my father was buried,
it was raining, and I was touching myself,
thinking of Debbie, who wrote on our prom picture
that she would never forget the night we had.

Jenny just called to say
it is raining in Seattle now, too.
My mind is full of rain, and my heart of dust and longing.

Downpour

Surely you've been there,
walking on a street at the start of your twenties
under a downpour so sudden you're drenched
moments after dismissing that first drop
as mere air conditioner spit on your skin.
Around you, people rush to cluster
beneath awnings and the narrow shelter of doorways.
But, though you can hear your mother's voice
urging you to follow,
it isn't cold, you haven't far, and in truth,
you like the weight of your sopping hair
and how your clothes cling
as though pressed by the flat of a hand.
So, while people have begun to stare, a man leers
and a child says, "she crazy", nudging his mother,
you keep your stride beneath the sky
of this particular day, taking what it has to offer.

Acts of Faith

Friends describe colors to me:
trumpets are red they say,
clarinets purple, and oranges
taste like orange. I believe them—
no reason not to.

I buy books to read with equipment for the blind.
It is an act of faith. In the bookstore
all the pages are blank.

At the checkout counter, I pay
with a bill that, earlier,
the grocer said was a twenty.
Or I sign a blank slip,
wherever the cashier tells me.

"No big deal," I say to myself,
walking out the door.
"Nobody knows everything."
I smell the city—oil and brown.
The yellow sun shines lemonade,
which means the sky must be blue.

Ignoring the Apples

Her name is the beginning
of night. Mornings, she nibbles
on figs; draws, stick scraping earth;
watches for animals in cumulus
clouds. Afternoons are a hum
of meal preparation, peaches
that bleed sweetness; greens she
splits at a touch; nuts that shell
themselves. Her husband sighs
as he eats; breathes compliments;
rests his head on her stomach
to invent words. Finally the sky turns
plum-colored. God's tree becomes
shadow. A hiss in the air whispers
Eve. Or maybe it's *please*.

Adam's Deposition

We would lie
naked in sunwarmth,
talking hour upon hour,
our slack language
sweet as honeysuckle
on an almost aimless breeze.
Or we would walk all afternoon,
through grasses, stopping
only to eat of the garden.

And then, one day, while I dozed,
happy just to know she was near,
she came to me, her mind different—
how can I put it?—humming
like bees in clover, ready
for something untasted.

I had never heard her so awake,
so full of purpose and wonder.
I wanted to go where she went,
and so yes, I said, let us both
put it into our mouths.

Abraham's Hand

As though they were your own,
you know the sloping lines
and dry patches in your father's palms.
The calluses on his fingertips
like small coins hidden in the skin.
You know the crevice of a scar
between two right knuckles
and the dark pattern of hairs above.
He has given you tools and shaped
your fingers around them
to show you their uses,
mussed your hair and passed you
countless baskets of bread.
As a baby you clutched his rough finger
the way birds wrap their feet
around branches to stand.
Now he comes to you saying,
"Walk with me to the mountain"
and holds out his hand.

The Price

Father told me nothing
of his plan and God's for me
when he shook me from sleep
long before the animals awoke.
I was old enough now, he said,
to carry our supplies up the mountain
to the clearing and the thicket.

I only learned of the plan as we came back down,
him singing lustily to God,
drunk with relief,
crazy happy.

I'm glad he doesn't tell
how I tried to run
when I realized what was happening,
how I cried as I lost
my fight against the lashes
to the altar he had improvised.

He only tells of the Lord's loving-kindness,
of his own unflagging faith, the miracle
of a ram appearing just in time from nowhere.
"Jehovah is great," he cries
after each time he tells the story.
I nod to keep him happy,
but at night I lie awake.

Exodus

A woman has painted her doorpost
with blood so that now, in gray half light,
she shakes a small shoulder,
pats a curved back, and her children
startle awake, allow themselves
to be rushed into clothes.
Trusting the hush, they quietly follow
as she walks with their father,
as they join a river of families
coursing from home. They walk and walk,
a block of bread dough on her back.
She is used to waking early, used to
hefting, carrying, hurrying tasks.
Such is the life they steal away from;
and she could almost feel light,
listening to the sound of her children's
feet beside her, breathing the baby's
sour milk head resting on her chest.
But she hears the cries of those
other mothers, the ones waking now
to the stiff unblinking bodies of their boys.
Joined by a thousand voices,
the wail rises, thicker than the dust
they kick up as they walk.
Can we let ourselves be loved by such a god?
She'd ask this of her husband
but she knows what he would say.
Adonai Echad. What choice do we have?

Providence

I met my girlfriend in yoga.
I was there on a whim.
Her class across town had been canceled.
"Meant to be," she laughed, six months later.
"Dumb luck," I said.

When the tsunami struck,
Thomas Goodpenny crossed himself
and thanked God for his charmed life—
the deal he was supposed to close in Sri Lanka
had already fallen through.

Finally, when pushed to the wall,
my mother admitted, "No,
I don't absolutely know
there's a heaven—nobody does—
but I don't want to take the chance by not believing."

I just shuffle the options:
take my dog in the car
and hope there's no accident,
or leave her at home
and pray for no fire.

Yet, last week at a writers' workshop,
the leader dumped a pile of cookie fortunes
in front of my girlfriend. "Take one," he said,
"and see if it doesn't somehow surprise your poem."
"Wait till you hear this, Mr. Dumb-luck,"
she whispered to me, tucking it into her pocket.
Back in her room she unfolded it:
"Stop searching forever; happiness is right next to you."
I thought she meant it for me.
She thought it was meant for her.

First Anniversary

Once, as a child, I had my father
close his eyes for a surprise
then, distractedly, walked him
into a wall. Now, guiding you,
I know to mention each curb, each
puddle to be stepped over, to place
your palm on the chipped rail
beside the subway stairs before
I follow you down. All the while,
the tip of your folded white cane
peeks from the side pocket of your pack
like something inner and exposed.
We've spent this year learning one
another. One night, you asked the color
of my hair then repeated the word brown,
an abstract fact to be memorized.
The dark strands were splayed
on your chest as I listened
to the beat beneath skin and rib
and thought about trust, your life
in your hand given over to mine.

Why I'm So Mixed Up about Rhyme

Because I am just as mixed up about home—
whether I want dinner every night
with the same people, who might be kind to me,
or just as easily start a fight.

And it's not just rhyme, but rhythm—
the way the two, combined, control and shape a line.
Soon lines make stanzas, as walls make rooms and houses
that keep horses from coming in to dine.

But isn't it good sometimes to force
things to go where they wouldn't otherwise?
In the apparent safety of a partner and a home,
isn't there always a surprise?

Oh, I am a wild pony galloping across Chincoteague—
governed only by my desires, unencumbered by familial ties—
and simultaneously a man with the same woman every night,
my domesticated hand resting between her thighs.

There among the Haves

A girl with one prosthetic leg dances
at a club in short skirt and heels
on the cover of *SundayStyles*, her
silver thigh textured like sequins,
hair over her face, not to hide
but she's lost in that song.
I tape her photo next to my desk,
remember the morning I had you
touch my calves, the right thin
with palsy, the other, full and strong.
That same day we kissed like teens
in a New York café, your guide dog
curled like a throw rug at our feet.
"Anyone else making out?" you asked.
"Just us," I said, eyeing an indifferent
crowd. And there, among the haves,
those with sight, with matching limbs,
you whispered that my breasts spell
a perfect C in braille. So this is how
it feels, I thought, to inherit the earth,
how it feels loving one of my own.

Questions

It was you, Darling,
oh it was most definitely you.
Even in a dream, I know
the exact angle of our noses in kissing.
I know the fragrant mélange
of fish and flower that is
your olfactory fingerprint
in the nakedness of love.

So it was strange, then,
that you were my sister in this dream,
this dream where we giggled and worried that our father
might innocently, imprudently, peek in.

Not my sister, to be precise,
but in the role of sister.
I've been asking myself all day, why.
Why with all the wanting,
no reduction in our usual desire,
would you be made a sister?
To send me back to my real sister
with better than I've given her before?
To show me what long-time lived-in love looks like?

And what if we all had sisters
who would fall asleep with us?
Would we learn earlier to love?

Come, my Love,
isn't it time we were family?

Additional Acknowledgments

"Abraham's Hand" was republished in *Your Daily Poem*, June 19, 2010.

"Hemiplegia II" as "Hemiplegia" appeared in the anthology, *Beauty is a Verb: The New Poetry of Disability*, edited by Jennifer Bartlett, Sheila Black, and Michael Northen, Cinco Puntos Press, 2011.

"When the Man You Love Is a Blind Man" appeared in *Challenges for the Delusional*, edited by Christine Malvasi, Jane Street Press, 2012, and was republished in *Wordgathering*.

"Retelling," "Hemiplegia I," "In Rockaway," "Border Song," "Eighteen," "Hemiplegia II," "When the Man You Love is a Blind Man," "Downpour," "First Anniversary," and "There among the Haves" appeared in the poetry collection, *Geode*, Main Street Rag, 2014.

"In Rockaway" and "Donner Lake" appeared in the chapbook, *Left Standing*, Finishing Line Press, 2005.

"When We Were Four," "Visitations of Abandonment," "A Blind Boy's First Glimpse of Heaven," "All Day, New Friends," "My Excuse," "Vigilance and Dissembling" and "Acts of Faith," appeared in the poetry collection, *School for the Blind*, Poets Wear Prada, 2015.

"Acts of Faith" can be heard on *Audio Chapbook*, a compact disc of poetry by Daniel Simpson and David Simpson, produced and released by the twins in 2007.

Special thanks to Juan Alberto Pérez for allowing us to place his beautiful painting, *Dancing in Blue*, on the cover of this book.

Ona Gritz's poetry collection, *Geode*, was a finalist for the 2013 *Main Street Rag Poetry Book Award*. Her poems have appeared in *Ploughshares, Bellevue Literary Review, Seneca Review, Beauty Is a Verb: The New Poetry of Disability* and many other journals and anthologies. Ona's chapbook of poems, *Left Standing*, was published by Finishing Line Press in 2005. Her memoir, *On the Whole: a story of mothering and disability* is available from Shebooks, an imprint of short ebooks by women, and as an audiobook from Audible. com. Ona recently ended a twelve-year tenure as a columnist for *Literary Mama*. She also served, along with her husband Daniel Simpson, as poetry editor for *Referential Magazine*.

§

Daniel Simpson's collection of poems, *School for the Blind*, was published by Poets Wear Prada in 2014. His work has appeared in *Prairie Schooner, The Cortland Review, Hampden-Sydney Poetry Review, Passager, The Atlanta Review, The Louisville Review* and *The New York Times*, among others. Cinquo Puntos Press published his essay "Line Breaks the Way I See Them" and four of his poems in *Beauty Is a Verb: The New Poetry of Disability*, now in its second printing. The recipient of a Fellowship in Literature from the Pennsylvania Council on the Arts, he served, along with his wife, Ona Gritz, as poetry editor for *Referential Magazine*, an online literary journal. His blog, *Inside the Invisible*, can be found at insidetheinvisible.wordpress.com.

CPSIA information can be obtained
at www.ICGtesting.com
Printed in the USA
BVOW09s0133280917
496071BV00002B/202/P